SILLY STORIES

Silly Stories

Andrew Matthews

Illustrated by Tony Ross

**A Dolphin
Paperback**

for
Gill, Jim and Rose

Published in paperback in 1995
by Orion Children's Books
a division of the Orion Publishing Group Ltd
Orion House
5 Upper St Martin's Lane
London WC2H 9EA
First published in Great Britain in 1994
by Orion Children's Books

Second impression 1996
Third impression 1997

A catalogue record for this book is
available from the British Library.
Printed in Great Britain
ISBN 1 85881 098 1

Contents

Introduction   6

Map of Waffam   8

1. The Three Wishes   11

2. Lazy Jack   17

3. Three Foolish Friends   23

4. A Search for Sillies   31

5. The Hobyahs   38

6. The Goose Supper that Wasn't   45

7. Who Had the Silliest Husband?   50

8. The Leaning Sheep   58

9. The Vinegars   65

10. Dan and his Brains   74

11. Stone Soup   81

12. The Boasting Competition   87

Outroduction   95

Introduction

Waffam looked like a perfect country village (you can see a map of it over the page). Ducks dibbed in the pond on the village green, carts rattled across the cobbles in the market square and the church clock rang out the hours on a sleepy-sounding bell. Swallows built nests in the roofs of thatched cottages in summer and children built snowmen in the cottage gardens in winter. Anyone who visited Waffam for the first time thought it was a pretty, peaceful place.

   They couldn't have been more wrong. The village looked quiet enough, but some of the people who lived there were a different matter. Silliness had spread through the village like bindweed in a flower-bed. In fact, the villagers were so used to mad goings-on that if the mayor put his clothes on back to front, or a farmer's wife slept in a sty so that her prize pig could sleep in a feather bed, no one gave it much thought.

"That's just the way we do things round here," visitors were told.

And so Waffam became a place that people in other villages told tales about, and those that heard the tales went to see for themselves if they were true. They didn't stay in Waffam long, though. The silliness was catching and after only a few hours there, they found themselves doing the most peculiar things.

So you'd better take care when you read these stories. . . .

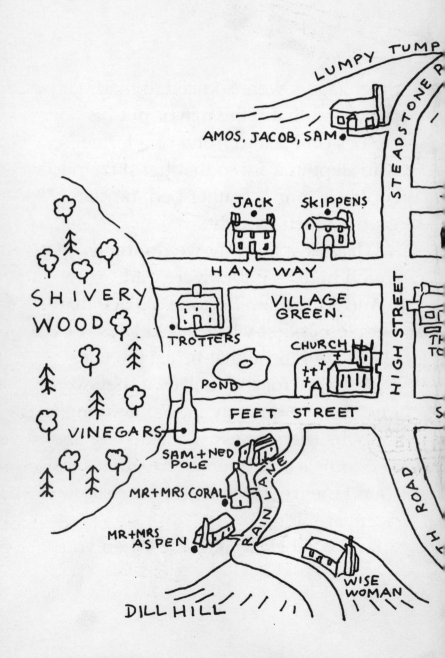

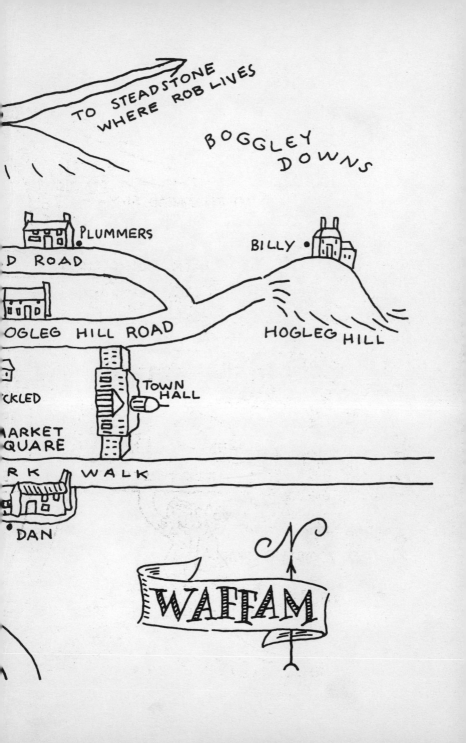

1

The Three Wishes

Mr Skippen and his wife lived in Waffam.
They owned a cottage in Hay Way near the
village green. When people passed by the
cottage, they often heard the sound of
shouting, because the Skippens argued from
morning till night, and they often argued in
their sleep as well. If Mr Skippen said one
thing, his wife would say the opposite, and if
they weren't arguing about this or that, they
were sure to be arguing about the other.

One afternoon, as Mr Skippen was walking
on the green, he heard a splashing and a
screeching that sounded like a parrot falling
into a bowl of milk.

Mr Skippen turned, and saw an old
woman in the pond. She was thrashing and
squealing and crying fit to burst.

"Help!" she screamed. "Help! I can't swim!"

Mr Skippen hurried over to the pond and
held out his walking stick. The old woman
caught hold of it and Mr Skippen
pulled her safe on to dry land.

As the old woman
stood dripping in
front of him, Mr
Skippen noticed
how ugly she was.
Her nose was as
curved and
pointed as the
new moon and
there was a
wart the size
of a raspberry
on her chin.

"However did you manage to fall into the pond?" Mr Skippen asked.

"I must have gone to sleep and fallen off my broomstick as it was flying along," the old woman replied.

"B-broomstick?" said Mr Skippen. "Flying? Are you a w-w-witch?"

"I certainly am!" said the old woman. "And to show you how grateful I am that you saved my life, I'm going to use my magic to grant you three wishes."

Mr Skippen hurried home to tell his wife the good news, but she didn't seem pleased.

"Only three wishes?" she said. "You should have asked her for more while you had the chance, you fool."

"Hold your tongue and get my supper ready while I think about what to wish for," said Mr Skippen. "What are we having for supper, anyway?"

"Cabbage soup, the same as we always

have," said Mrs Skippen.

"Cabbage soup? Bah, I'm sick of the stuff!"
Mr Skippen grumbled. "I wish I had a nice
big sizzling sausage for my supper."

No sooner had he said this, than there was
a loud CLANG! and the frying pan flew off
the shelf on to the table. In the frying pan
sizzled a nice big sausage.

"Now look what you've done!" scolded
Mrs Skippen. "You and your big mouth! We
could have had a palace! We could have had
gold and jewels – but oh, no! You had to go
and waste a wish on a stupid sausage!"

"They're my wishes, so keep your nose out
of my business!" snapped Mr Skippen. "I
wish this sausage was stuck on the end of
your nose! That would teach you a lesson!"

As soon as he had spoken there was a
loud PING! and the sausage hopped out of
the frying pan and stuck itself right on the
end of Mrs Skippen's nose.

"Oh, very nice, I'm sure!" she said, putting her hands on her hips. "How am I going to manage with a sausage on the end of my nose? What will the neighbours say?"

"Stop nagging and come here," said Mr Skippen. "I'll cut the sausage off with this carving knife."

"You'll do no such thing!" said Mrs Skippen. "You'll keep your hands off my nose, thank you very much! And if the sound of sizzling keeps you awake all night, serves you right! When I think of all the things you could have wished for –!"

"Oh, do stop moaning, woman!" said Mr Skippen, putting his hands over his ears. "I wish I'd never had any wishes in the first place!"

The instant the last word left his lips there was a loud POP! and the sausage vanished, and Mr and Mrs Skippen were left with nothing.

They argued about whose fault it was for the rest of their days.

2
Lazy Jack

A bit further along Hay Way, Jack lived with his widowed mother. Jack's mother took in washing and ironing and worked hard to earn a bit of money, but Jack didn't do any work at all. He was so lazy, he wouldn't even feed himself. When they had peas, his mother would use a spoon to flick them across the room into Jack's mouth.

One Monday, Jack's mother could stand it no more. She told Jack that if he didn't start earning his keep, she'd turn him out of the house. So on Tuesday, Jack got himself a day's work at Palm Farm, and the farmer, Mr Palmer, paid him a penny. Because he'd never earned wages before, Jack didn't know what to do with the penny. He held it tightly in his hand, but it slipped out of his grip and lost itself as he was crossing a stream on his way home.

"You silly boy!" his mother told him. "You should have put it in your pocket!"

"You know best, Mother," said Jack.

On Wednesday, Jack went to work for Howard the Cowherd, who gave him a big jug of milk for his wages. Jack put the jug in his pocket, but by the time he got home all the milk had sloshed out of it and he was wetter than a fish's slippers.

"You silly boy!" said his mother. "You should have carried it home on your head!"

"I won't be so silly next time," said Jack.

Thursday came, and Jack got a job at Mary's Dairy. Mary paid him with a big slab of butter. Jack put the butter on his head and off he went. It was such a hot day that by the

time he reached home, the butter had melted
into his hair and made it as greasy as the
inside of an old frying pan.

"You silly boy!" said his mother. "You
should have carried it home in your hands!"

"I won't make that mistake again," said
Jack.

On Friday, Jack worked for Mr Laker the
Baker, who gave him a handsome tomcat.
Jack carried the cat in his hands, but the cat
wriggled so much it was like carrying a furry
python. Before he'd gone very far, old Tom

gave him such a bite with his sharp teeth and
such a scratch with his sharp claws that Jack
let him go.

"You silly boy!" said his mother. "You
should have tied a rope around it and
walked it home!"

"Of course I should! You're quite right,"
said Jack.

On Saturday, Jack went to work for Mr
Mopp at the butcher's shop. Mr Mopp was so
pleased with him that he gave him a string of
sausages for his pay. Jack tied a
rope around the sausages and
walked them home. By
the time he got there,
the sausages were
covered in so much
grit and dust that
they had to be
thrown away.

"You silly boy!" said his mother. "You should have carried them home over your shoulders!"

"Whatever you say, Mother," said Jack.

The following Monday, Jack went to work for Mr Howman the Ploughman, and Mr Howman gave him a donkey. The donkey kicked and brayed, but at last Jack got it over his shoulders and staggered home.

On the way, Jack met a couple of strangers – a farmer and his little daughter. The daughter had been ill and since her illness she'd been as miserable as rain in a rusty tin. The farmer had taken his daughter to the best doctors in the land, and they'd all told him the only thing that would make her properly better was to have a good laugh. The farmer had heard about how silly the people of Waffam were and he was bringing her on a visit in the hope that something would make her chuckle.

Well, when she saw Jack stumbling along the road with a donkey over his shoulders, and the donkey's ears and legs waggling about in the air, the girl laughed until tears filled her eyes and she was better at once.

The farmer was so overjoyed, he gave Jack a big bag of gold.

"You ride home on the donkey, lad, and keep a tight hold on that bag of money," said the farmer.

"Right you are. I'll do that," said Jack.

And he made no mistakes this time, I can tell you.

3

Three Foolish Friends

The Cuckoo Hedge

On top of Lumpy Tump, the hill just outside Waffam, lived three friends named Amos, Jacob and Sam. They thought they were a crafty trio, but in fact they were as silly as silly could be.

One spring morning they were out in their garden when they heard a cuckoo calling from a rose bush.

"Wonderful!" said Amos, clasping his hands together in joy. "I love to hear a cuckoo. It cheers me up no end!"

"Me too!" agreed Jacob. "Isn't it a shame that the cuckoo flies away in September? It would be nice to hear it all year round."

"Nothing simpler!" said Sam. "We'll plant a hedge around the cuckoo and keep it in."

So they did. They planted a big hedge around the rose bush where the cuckoo sang. They watered the hedge every day and kept it neat and tidy with a pair of garden clippers.

Of course, when September came, the cuckoo flew off to follow the sunshine south. When Amos and Jacob found the cuckoo had gone, they were disappointed, but Sam said, "Cheer up! We'll try again next year, and this time we'll plant a taller hedge!"

This was such a good idea that Amos threw his hat on the ground and Jacob slapped himself on the knee.

"Sam," he said, "when it comes to being wise, there's no one to beat you!"

Amos's Cheeses

Amos had made three big cheeses and he decided to sell them at market. He loaded the cheeses into a backpack and set off early.

Now the backpack had a hole in it, and the cheeses were so heavy that the hole got bigger and bigger as Amos walked down Lumpy Tump. He knew nothing about this until the hole got big enough for the cheeses to drop through. They fell on to the road and went rolling down the hill towards Waffam.

"Just look at that!" chuckled Amos. "Those cheeses are in such a hurry to get to market, they can't wait for me to carry them and they've gone on ahead by themselves!" He cupped his hands round his mouth and shouted, "Meet me underneath the church clock at two!"

When the cheeses reached the bottom of the hill, they went all over the place. One fell into a muddy ditch, one rolled into a field and was eaten by a goat, and one bounced on a stone and ended up stuck in a tree.

Amos reached the church clock just as it was striking two, but there was no sign of the cheeses, so he sat down and waited.

After an hour or so, who should come strolling along but his pals, Jacob and Sam.

"What are you doing here?" they asked.

Amos told them about the cheeses.

"Are you sure they knew the way to the church?" asked Sam. "They were only young."

"That's the trouble with the young!" sighed Jacob. "They're always rushing ahead without thinking."

Sam and Jacob walked off. Poor Amos sat in the churchyard all night, but the cheeses never turned up.

"They must have got lost, poor things!" Amos told himself as he trudged home. "Next time, I'll draw a map and show my cheeses where the church is!"

The Moon in the Pond

Jacob was out for a stroll one evening when he passed the village pond and saw the moon in the water.

"Bless us and save us, the moon's fallen into the pond!" he said, and he raced home as fast as he could. "Amos!" he called. "Sam! Come quickly, the moon's fallen out of the sky and it's landed in the village pond."

"Are you sure?" gasped Amos.

"Come and see for yourself!" said Jacob.

Off went the three of them, and sure enough, there was the moon in the water.

"This is serious," said Sam. "If the moon stays in there, it'll drown, and if there's no moon, then how will people find their way around at night? We must rescue it from the pond, dry it and get it back into the sky right away."

They ran back to their cottage. Amos grabbed a shovel, Jacob got a rake and Sam found an old net he used to catch tadpoles with when he was a lad. They returned to the pond and set to work.

And hard work it was. Amos tried to shovel the water away from the moon, but no matter how much water he shovelled out there was still plenty left to fill in the hole his shovel made. Jacob tried to rake the moon out of the water, but the moon kept on wobbling and slipping through the teeth of his rake. Sam just couldn't seem to dip his net deep enough to catch the moon.

After a long while, Amos, Jacob and Sam were so tired that they fell down beside the pond and took a rest.

"Hey!" cried Sam, lying on his back and pointing at the sky. "We did it!"
Amos and Jacob looked up and there was the moon, safe and sound among the stars.

"It was a lucky thing I came along when I did!" said Jacob.

"It was lucky we were here to help you," said Amos.

"It's lucky we're all so clever," said Sam, "or we wouldn't have known what to do."

So Amos, Jacob and Sam went off home together, certain that they had saved the moon and certain that they were the three cleverest men in the whole of Waffam.

4

A Search for Sillies

Mr and Mrs Plummer lived in Toad Road with their daughter Polly. Polly was pretty, but she was as foolish as she was pretty and her mother and father were worse than she was.

Polly was being courted by Tam Dunn. Tam lived in Steadstone, a village on the other side of the Boggley Downs. Steadstone was nothing like Waffam – the people who lived there had a bit of sense. One day, young Tam turned up at Polly's house to ask for her hand in marriage.

"Put the kettle on for a cup of tea, Polly," said Mrs Plummer. "Talking about weddings is thirsty work."

After a long time had gone by and Polly still hadn't come back, Mrs Plummer went to the kitchen to find her. There stood Polly with a frown on her face. She'd filled the kettle so full that the water had overflowed into the sink, and now the sink was full, so the water was pouring on to the floor.

"What are you doing?" asked Mrs Plummer.

"I was wondering what to call my first baby after Tam and I are married," Polly said. "All the names I can think of already belong to someone."

"Hmm, that's a problem!" said Mrs Plummer, scratching her head.

After a long time had gone by and Polly and her mother still hadn't come back, Mr Plummer went into the kitchen to find them. There stood Polly and Mrs Plummer, with frowns on their faces and water up to their ankles.

"What are you doing?" asked Mr Plummer.

"We're wondering what to call the children Polly and Tam will have after they get married," said Mrs Plummer. "All the names we can think of already belong to someone."

"Hmm! That's a problem," said Mr Plummer, rubbing his chin.

After a long time had gone by without Polly, Mrs Plummer or Mr Plummer coming back, Tam went into the kitchen to find them. There they stood with frowns on their faces and water up to their knees, wiggling their toes inside their soggy socks.

"What are you doing?" said Tam. "Can't you see the kitchen's flooded?"

"Yes," said Mr Plummer, "but after you and Polly get married, what are you going to call your children? All the names we can think of already belong to someone."

Tam could hardly believe his ears. "Well, I was told you were silly, but I didn't know you were *that* silly!" he said. "I'm off. When I've met three people sillier than you lot, I'll come back and marry Polly, but not before!"

Off went Tam down the road, and after he'd walked for a good while he saw a man sitting outside a cottage. The man had a bowl in one hand and a fork in the other. Great tears were rolling down his face.

"What's wrong?" asked Tam.

"I'm starving!" sobbed the man. "I've cooked myself a lovely bowl of soup, but when I try to eat it, it falls right through my fork!"

"Try using a spoon," said Tam.

"What a good idea! I never thought of that!" said the man.

Tam carried on down the road. "Well, that's one person who's sillier than the Plummers," he said to himself.

The road ran through a grove of oak trees. Tam hadn't gone far when he saw a man trying to make a pig climb a ladder that was propped against one of the trees.

"What are you up to?" asked Tam.

"I'm trying to feed this pig some acorns,"

said the man, "but the stupid animal won't climb the ladder to reach them."

"Why don't you climb the ladder yourself and shake the acorns on to the ground for the pig?" said Tam.

"What a good idea! I never thought of that!" said the man.

Tam carried on down the road. "That's two people sillier than the Plummers," he said to himself.

A bit further on, he came across a man who was jumping up and down in front of a pair of trousers tied to a tree branch.

"Need any help?" asked Tam.

"I just can't get these trousers on!" said the man. "No matter how high I jump, I just can't land inside them!"

"If you held them in your hands," said Tam, "you could step into them one leg at a time."

"What a good idea! I never thought of

that!" said the man.

Now Tam had found three people sillier than the Plummers, he returned to their house.

"You weren't long, lad," said Mr Plummer.

"No. The world's a far sillier place than I thought," said Tam.

So Polly and Tam were married and when they had children, Polly made up names for them – Tangerine, Sausage and Donk.

5

The Hobyahs

On the west side of Waffam lay Shivery Wood. Near Shivery Wood stood a thatched cottage, and in that cottage Mr and Mrs Trotter lived with their little dog, Turpin.

Every night when the clock struck twelve, the Hobyahs would come out of the wood on tiptoe, rolling their eyes, and licking their lips, and clicking their claws, whispering:

"We'll break down the door
with a bash and a crack!
We'll carry the Trotters
away in a sack!"

But every night Turpin heard the Hobyahs coming, and he barked so loudly that he frightened them away.

Mr and Mrs Trotter knew nothing about the Hobyahs, but they knew Turpin was barking because it woke them up.

"If that dog of ours doesn't stop barking in the middle of the night," said Mr Trotter, "I shall have to take off his legs."

That night, just after the clock struck twelve, the Hobyahs came out of the wood on tiptoe, rolling their eyes, and licking their lips, and clicking their claws, and whispering:

"We'll break down the door with a bash and a crack! We'll carry the Trotters away in a sack!"

As soon as Turpin heard the Hobyahs, he barked as loudly as he could and frightened them away. But Mr Trotter woke up and got out of bed and he took off Turpin's legs.

"And if that doesn't do the trick, I'll have to unscrew your head!" said Mr Trotter.

Well, the next night, just after the clock struck twelve, the Hobyahs came out of the wood on tiptoe, rolling their eyes, and licking their lips, and clicking their claws, and whispering:

"We'll break down the door with a bash and a crack! We'll carry the Trotters away in a sack!"

Turpin heard the Hobyahs and he barked loudly to frighten them away, but he woke up his master. Mr Trotter got out of bed and he unscrewed Turpin's head.

"That'll fix you and your barking once and for all!" he said.

Well, the next night, just after midnight, the Hobyahs came out of the wood on tiptoe, rolling their eyes, and licking their lips, and clicking their claws and whispering:

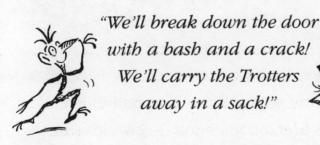

"We'll break down the door
with a bash and a crack!
We'll carry the Trotters
away in a sack!"

This time, there was no barking from Turpin to see them off, so the Hobyahs

41

broke down the door of the cottage with a bash and a crack, and they popped Mrs Trotter into a sack, and they carried her back to their cave in the forest, and they hung the sack from a nail in the wall.

They didn't catch Mr Trotter, because he hid himself under the bed. As soon as he was sure the Hobyahs had gone, Mr Trotter came out of hiding.

"I've been so stupid!" he said. "Turpin was keeping the Hobyahs away, and I went and took off his legs, and unscrewed his head. Now the Hobyahs have taken away my wife and I don't know what I shall do!"

Mr Trotter went to find Turpin and he stuck his legs back on and screwed his head back. Turpin started sniffing the ground, and when he smelled the Hobyahs, he growled.

Off he went into Shivery Wood, following the scent, with Mr Trotter close behind him. When they reached the Hobyahs' cave the Hobyahs were out digging turnips.

Turpin's clever nose soon found Mrs Trotter in the sack.

As soon as she was free, Mrs Trotter gave her husband a hug and said, "Back home as fast as we can! The Hobyahs will be here any minute!"

Mr and Mrs Trotter hurried home, but Turpin hopped into the sack and waited. Before long, he heard the Hobyahs' tippy toes, and rolly eyes, and licky lips, and clicky claws, and their voices whispering:

"Ha, ha, ha, ha!
Hee, hee, hee, hee!
We'll have Mrs Trotter
with turnips for tea!"

When the Hobyahs were all in the cave,
Turpin jumped out of the sack, snarling and
barking and biting.

And the Hobyahs ran. They ran out of the
wood, through the village, over the top of
Lumpy Tump and all the way to the
seashore. Then they dived into the sea and
swam down to the bottom, and there they
stayed.

And that's why there are no Hobyahs in
Shivery Wood nowadays.

6

The Goose Supper That Wasn't

Sam and Ned Pole lived with their mother on Rain Lane, just round the corner from Waffam Church. Mother had a difficult time keeping the peace between her sons – Sam and Ned couldn't agree about anything. If Sam said that a jug of milk was half-full, then Ned said it was half-empty. When Ned said that the weather looked fine, Sam said he thought it would rain. Not a day went by without the two of them squabbling over something or other.

One morning, Sam and Ned went hunting.

As they passed by the village green, they
noticed a fine fat goose swimming in the
pond.

"Phew!" sighed Sam, licking his lips. "If
we can catch that goose, we'll have a super
supper! There's nothing better than roast
goose stuffed with plums! I can taste it
already!"

"Roast goose?" said Ned. "Boiled goose
has got far more flavour! Boiled goose with
chestnut dumplings is the best dinner in
the world!"

"Boiled goose
is awful!"
said Sam.
"No it isn't!"
said Ned.
"Yes it is!"

And they were soon squabbling again. Just
as it seemed they might come to blows, Sam

said, "Let's go home and ask Mother. She knows a thing or two about cooking."

"There's no point in asking her, she'll only agree with me!" said Ned.

"No she won't!" said Sam.

"Yes she will!"

And they were at it again. They squabbled all the way back to their garden gate. Mrs Pole was sitting on the front doorstep, shelling peas into a bowl.

"What's the best way to cook a goose, Mother?" asked Sam. "I say roast it, Ned says boil it."

Mrs Pole knew that if she agreed with Sam, Luke would be offended, and if she agreed with Luke, Sam would be offended. After a bit of quick thinking, she said, "You're both right. The best way to cook a goose is to boil it for a bit and then roast it in the oven for a bit."

So, that squabble was settled. Sam and Ned shook on it. They went back to the pond, but by the time they got there, the goose had flown away.

"Oh, well!" sighed Sam as they returned home empty-handed. "We'll have to have cauliflower cheese for supper instead of goose!"

"You mean macaroni cheese, don't you?" said Ned. "I saw some macaroni on the kitchen shelf yesterday."

"And I saw a cauliflower in the pantry,"
said Sam, "so that means Mother is going to
cook cauliflower cheese."

"No it doesn't!" said Ned.

"Yes it does!" said Sam.

In the end, they were so busy arguing that
they didn't notice *what* they had for supper.

7

Who Had the
Silliest Husband?

Mrs Coral lived next door to the Poles, and
Mrs Aspen lived next door to Mrs Coral on
the other side. Mr Aspen and Mr Coral
worked together and got along fine, but Mrs
Aspen and Mrs Coral were always
disagreeing about whose husband was most
silly.

"My husband's far more stupid than
yours," Mrs Aspen said. "He puts the baby's
nappy on round its head, and one day he
tried to walk into the garden from an upstairs
window, because he thought it would be

quicker than going downstairs and using the door."

"Call that stupid?" snorted Mrs Coral. "My husband tried to keep sunlight in jars to save on candles, and only last week when I sent him out to buy a bag of flour, he came back with a hen that won't lay any eggs."

"I bet I can prove my husband is more stupid than yours," said Mrs Aspen.

"Bet you can't," said Mrs Coral.

Mrs Aspen gave it a bit of thought, and just before her husband came in from work, she got out her knitting needles and pretended she was knitting. She didn't even look up when her husband came in. He stared at her for a while with his mouth wide open, and then he said,

"Did you know that you're sitting there knitting nothing?"

"I'm not knitting nothing!" Mrs Aspen declared. "I'm using a new kind of wool that's so fine, nobody can see it. I'm going to make a coat for you."

"Well, if you hadn't told me I wouldn't have known anything was there!" said her husband.

After an hour of pretending to knit, Mrs Aspen threw down her needles and held out her empty hands.

"There!" she said. "It's ready for you to try on."

She made her husband take off his coat, and pretended to help him on with the invisible one.

"It's not very warm," said Mr Aspen.

"That's because it's so fine," Mrs Aspen

replied. "It's not an everyday coat, you know. You must keep it for best."

"Everybody will be jealous when I'm wearing the coat they can't see!" said Mr Aspen. "I bet they'll all talk about me!"

"They'll talk about you, all right,," said his wife. "Especially when you wear the trousers I'm going to make you out of the same wool!"

Meanwhile, next door, Mr Coral had just come home from work. Mrs Coral looked at him and shook her head.

"You look terrible," she said. "I'd go to bed right away if I were you."

"And there I was thinking how fine I felt!" said Mr Coral. "But you know best, dear. If I look as bad as all that, maybe I'm sickening for something."

"You need a good night's sleep," said Mrs Coral. "If you don't get a proper rest, there'll be no hope for you."

Poor Mr Coral went straight off to bed, but he worried so much about being ill that he didn't sleep a wink.

"You're looking worse, I reckon," Mrs Coral said the next morning. "I'll make you a herb drink, but it's too late if you ask me."

"If you say so, dear," said Mr Coral, trembling with fear.

He stayed in bed all day. At noon, Mrs Coral brought him a bowl of broth.

"I'm feeling a lot better now, dear," said Mr Coral.

"Well, you're looking worse," Mrs Coral told him.

She told him the same thing when she brought him a cup of tea later, and in the evening, she knelt down beside his bed and burst into tears.

"Whatever's the matter?" asked Mr Coral.

"You're dead," came the reply.

"No!" said Mr Coral. "Honestly, I feel fine.

I'll just get up and make myself a bit of supper."

"You'll do no such thing!" said Mrs Coral. "I'm not having a corpse in my kitchen. You just lie there quiet while I go to see the undertaker."

"If you say so, dear," Mr Coral murmured.

Next morning, Mrs Coral told her husband to lie down in a coffin, and then the undertaker's men carried the coffin down to the churchyard, where all their friends and neighbours were waiting.

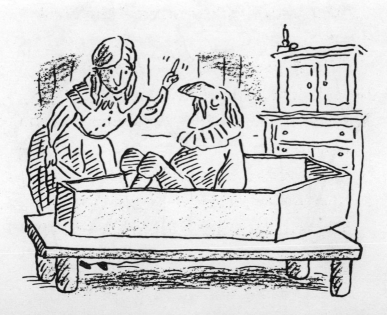

The last person to arrive was Mr Aspen. As far as anyone could see, he wasn't wearing any clothes at all. Everybody burst out laughing.

"What's going on?" Mr Coral asked from inside his coffin. "Somebody open the lid and let me have a look, I could do with a good laugh."

When they heard a voice coming from the coffin, Mr Coral's friends stopped laughing and opened the lid.

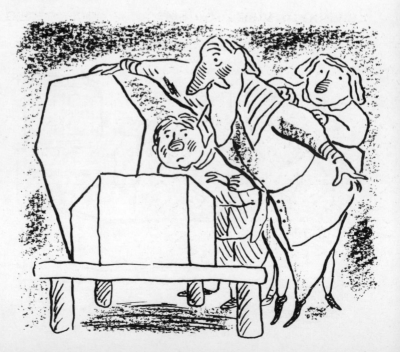

"What are you doing there, Coral, you old fool?" they asked. "You can't be buried – you're not dead yet. And what do you think you're playing at, Aspen? You'll catch your death of cold in a minute."

Well, Mrs Aspen and Mrs Coral owned up to what had been going on, but their friends and neighbours couldn't decide which of their husbands was the most foolish, and so the two women went on arguing about it. In fact, their argument went on for so long that they forgot what had started it, so they ended up as silly as their husbands.

8

The Leaning Sheep

He was a lad, was Billy – hair the colour of straw and eyes like pools of sky. Dreams made their homes in Billy's eyes the way swallows built nests under eaves.

Billy and his parents lived on a farm on the side of Hogleg Hill. Billy tried to help, but things he did had a habit of coming out wrong.

"You're useless, and that's a fact!" his father told him. "The day you do anything worthwhile, I'll eat my hat!"

Billy's father kept a flock of sheep, but when he herded the flock down on to the flat for driving to market in Waffam, he found that Hogleg Hill was so steep, all the sheep leaned to one side.

"No one's going to buy sheep that lean like this!" grumbled Billy's father. "A flock of useless sheep, a silly dreamer for a son – I must be the unluckiest man in the world!"

"You've still got your good health," his wife reminded him.

"That's true," said Billy's father, and then he sneezed. He sneezed himself out of the farmyard into the kitchen, he sneezed himself to the top of the stairs and then he sneezed himself straight into bed.

"You're too ill to go to market, so Billy must go instead," said Billy's mother.

"What, that woolly-headed good-for-nothing?" said Father. "He's about as much use as a hammer made of rainbows!"

"Going to market on his own could be the making of the lad," said Mother. "He might come back changed for the better."

"He couldn't come back changed for the worse!" Father groaned, burying his head in the pillows.

Bright and early next morning, Billy set off to Market Square, driving the flock of leaning sheep before him.

"So this is the wide world!" he said to himself as he strode along. "It's not as wide as I thought, but it's long. I've been walking down this road since I left home and I haven't come to the end of it yet!"

When Billy reached
Market Square, he put
the sheep into a pen and
waited. The first person
who came along was a man
with a big nose.

"What are they?" he said,
nodding at the pen.

"They're leaning sheep," said Billy.

"Leaning sheep?" laughed the man. "You
won't sell any of their meat, my lad. Who
wants to eat leaning mutton?"

After a while another man came along. He
had big ears.

"What kind of sheep have you got here?" he asked.

"Leaning sheep," said Billy.

"Leaning sheep?" laughed the man. "You won't sell any of their wool, my lad. Who can knit with leaning wool?"

Billy paid his laughter no mind. He was a lad who liked to keep cheerful. He whistled and dreamed the time away.

Late in the afternoon, a most peculiar man turned up. He had untidy hair, and he leaned over so far that his left ear was dusty from rubbing on the ground. He took one glance into Billy's pen and whooped for joy.

"Straight sheep!" he shouted. "Straight sheep at last! I've been searching for months and I've found nothing but leaning sheep until now! How much do you want for them?"

"If they're as rare as all that, they must be worth a lot," said Billy.

"Twenty gold pieces," said the old fellow, "take it or leave it."

"I'll take it, " said Billy.

So the deal was made – Billy got a bag of gold pieces and the man got the leaning sheep.

"Just a word before I go," the man said. "I couldn't help noticing that you've got a nasty lean to one side, lad. I think it must be catching, because most folks round here lean. I'd see a doctor and get yourself straightened out, then you can stand tall, like me."

"I might just do that," said Billy.

The man drove off the sheep, and Billy walked home, whistling happily.

And that night, Billy's father had to eat his hat. It tasted terrible!

9

The Vinegars

Mr and Mrs Vinegar lived in a huge vinegar bottle on Feet Street. They liked to keep the place tidy, but one day when they were cleaning, Mrs Vinegar bumped against the side of the bottle with the handle of the broom and smashed it into tinkling, glittering bits.

"That's the end of that house, then," said Mr Vinegar.

Mr and Mrs Vinegar gathered their few belongings in a sack, and Mr Vinegar carried the front door on his back.

"When we go to sleep tonight, we can shut the door and get a bit of peace," he told his wife.

They set off walking. When night came, they were in the middle of Shivery Wood.

"I can't walk another step!" declared Mrs Vinegar.

"Then we'll stay here for the night," said Mr Vinegar.

"I'm not sleeping on the ground!" said Mrs Vinegar. "The damp will get in my bones and make them creak."

So Mr Vinegar climbed a tree, put the front door across two branches and he and his wife went to sleep on that.

In the middle of the night, Mr Vinegar was woken up by voices talking under the tree. The voices belonged to three robbers who had been up to no good.

"There's ten gold pieces for you, Karl, and ten for you, Spike, and ten for me!" said the roughest voice of the three.

Mr Vinegar began to quiver with fear in case the robbers should look up and see him and his wife. And the quivering turned to a shivering, and the shivering turned to a shaking, and the shaking turned into a trembling so strong that it shook the door out from under Mr and Mrs Vinegar and sent it crashing to the ground.

"Look out, it's a trap!" shouted Karl.

The three robbers ran away so fast that their shoes couldn't keep up with them and had to follow on behind.

When Mr Vinegar climbed down from the tree, he found a bag on the ground. In that bag were thirty gold pieces, shining in the light of the moon.

"Come and see, Mrs Vinegar!" he shouted. "We're rich."

Down came Mrs Vinegar, and when she saw the money she jumped into the air and clicked her heels together.

"Mr Vinegar," she said, "tomorrow you must take that money to Market Square and buy a cow with it. We can milk the cow, and I can make butter and cheese from the milk and we can have a comfortable old age."

Mr Vinegar thought this was an excellent idea, so next morning, bright and early, he set off for Market Square and there he saw Farmer Palmer with a beautiful red cow.

"My wife and I would be the happiest people on earth if we had that cow," he told Farmer Palmer. "But all I've got is thirty gold pieces."

"That's strange!" Farmer Palmer cried. "Thirty gold pieces is just the price I wanted for the cow."

So Farmer Palmer got the money and Mr Vinegar got the cow, and he started back for Shivery Wood at once.

He hadn't gone very far when he met a man playing the bagpipes. Children followed him, dancing to his music, and people were dropping money into a hat that he held out to them.

Now if I could have a pair of bagpipes like that, thought Mr Vinegar, I could earn lots of money and I'd be the happiest man in the world.

He stopped the man and said, "My friend, I'd love to own that set of bagpipes of yours, but all I've got to offer in exchange is this red cow."

"That's amazing," said the man. "I was only just thinking how much I wanted a cow. We can do a swap, if you like."

So they did: the man walked off with the red cow and Mr Vinegar picked up the bagpipes, but when he tried to play them, they made a noise like a dozen cats down a well.

It was a cold morning, and by the time he left Waffam, Mr Vinegar's fingers were blue. After a while he met a man coming in the opposite direction, and he noticed that the man was wearing a pair of thick gloves.

"Oh, if only I had a pair of gloves like yours, I'd be the happiest man on earth!" said Mr Vinegar. "But I've got nothing to give in exchange except these bagpipes."

"Well, it's a funny old world and no mistake," said the man. "I was just going to market to see if I could buy some bagpipes."

So the man took the bagpipes and Mr Vinegar took the gloves. Now his hands were warm, but before long his legs began to ache. Just as the aching was at its worst, Mr Vinegar saw a man with a walking stick coming along the road.

"Oh, if only I had a good walking stick like yours, I'd be the happiest man that ever lived," said Mr Vinegar.

"I'm very fond of this stick, " said the man. "I wouldn't dream of parting with it for anything except a pair of good, thick gloves."

"Then take these!" cried Mr Vinegar.

So the man got the gloves, and Mr Vinegar got the walking stick and walked back to Shivery Wood, but on the way he dropped the stick as he was jumping across a stream, and it floated away.

Mr Vinegar found his wife waiting for him on an old stump.

"Didn't you buy a cow?" she asked.

"I certainly did!" said Mr Vinegar.

"Then where is it?" said Mrs Vinegar.

"I swapped it for a set of bagpipes."

"And where are the bagpipes?" said Mrs Vinegar.

"I swapped them for a pair of gloves."

"And where are the gloves?" said Mrs Vinegar.

"I swapped them for a walking stick."

"And where's the walking stick?" said Mrs Vinegar.

"I lost it in a stream," Mr Vinegar said.

When Mrs Vinegar heard this, she picked up her broom and gave her husband such a whack that he ended up in the middle of next week.

He's there now, waiting for the rest of us to catch up with him.

10

Dan and his Brains

Dan was a good-looking lad, but he was a bit silly and there was no getting away from it. In the end, Dan got so fed up with getting into scrapes and having folk laugh at him because he was foolish, he went to see the wise woman who lived on Dill Hill.

"I've come to see if you've got any brains for sale," said Dan.

"That depends," said the wise woman. "What sort of brains did you want?"

"Oh, just ordinary will do for me," said Dan.

The wise woman gave Dan a close look and scratched her chin.

"You bring me what you like best, and I'll see what I can do for you," she said.

"But I like all kinds of things," said Dan. "How will I know I've brought the right thing?"

"Because I'll ask you a riddle, and if you can tell me the answer, then you'll have brought me what you like best," said the wise woman.

Dan went home to his house in Stork Walk and he thought a bit, and in the morning he took his jar of honey off the shelf and carried it up the hill to the wise woman's cottage.

"There you are," said Dan, handing over the jar. "Honey's what I like best!"

"Is that so?" said the wise woman. "Then tell me, what can run with no legs?"

Well, Dan thought standing up, and he thought sitting down, but he couldn't think of the answer.

"No brains for you today, my lad," said the wise woman as she closed the door.

Dan went home and he thought a bit, and in the morning he popped his cat into a basket and carried it up the hill to the wise woman's cottage. The wise woman was outside, eating bread and honey.

"There you are," said Dan, handing over the bag. "My old cat Tiddles is what I like best."

"Is that so?" said the wise woman. "Then tell me, what's shiny and yellow, but isn't gold?"

Well, Dan thought with his cap on, and he thought with his cap off, but he couldn't think of the answer.

"No brains for you today, my lad," said the wise woman. She took Tiddles into her cottage and closed the door behind her.

Dan walked down the hill, slower than syrup running off a spoon. He was feeling low, and the further he walked, the lower he felt. So he sat at the side of the road and burst into tears.

Up came Daisy. She lived three houses away from Dan.

"Why are you crying?" she asked.

"I've given away the two things I like best, and I still haven't got any brains!" sobbed Dan.

"What are you talking about?" said Daisy.

She sat next to Dan and lent him a handkerchief to wipe away his tears, and he told her all about the wise woman.

"That's easy!" said Daisy. "I can answer those riddles!"

"What runs without legs, then?" asked Dan.

"Water," said Daisy.

"And what's shiny and yellow, but isn't gold?" asked Dan.

"The sun," said Daisy. "Come on, let's go and see the wise woman right away."

Up the hill they went, and there was the wise woman, sitting in her doorway with Tiddles curled up purring in her lap.

"Oh!" said the wise woman. "So it's Daisy you like best now, is it?"

"Er –," said Dan, blushing.

"Then tell me, what begins with no legs, then has two legs and ends up with four legs?" said the wise woman.

"A tadpole!" Daisy whispered in Dan's ear.

"Um, is it a tadpole?" asked Dan.

"It is," said the wise woman, "and you've got your brains, my lad."

"Where are they?" said Dan, searching his pockets.

"In Daisy's head," said the wise woman.

"I'd marry her quickly, if I were you, and then you can keep them."

And with that, she carried Tiddles into the cottage and shut the door behind her.

So Dan and Daisy got married, and Dan never had to worry about brains again, because Daisy had enough for them both.

11

Stone Soup

When Rob left his home in Steadstone, he had no job and no money – but he was as happy as a bobbing duck. He followed the road wherever it took him, living off his wits – and Rob could think faster than the flick of a cat's whisker.

One morning, Rob woke up to hear his insides grumbling and groaning.

"That's hunger talking," Rob said to himself. "If I don't eat soon, I'll get so thin that my shadow won't fit me any more."

Rob walked along the road until he came to Waffam. He walked up to the door of the nearest cottage and knocked loudly.

Mrs Skippen answered the door. She had such a big bandage tied round her nose that she had to peep over the top of it to see who was there. When she saw Rob, Mrs Skippen gave him a look that would have cracked a nut.

"Be off with you!" she said. "If you've come scrounging, you're out of luck."

"Madam," said Rob, "all I want is some boiling water so I can make myself some stone soup."

"Stone soup?" cried the woman.

"That's right," said Rob. He reached into his pocket and brought out a stone that he'd picked up at the side of the road. "With a drop of hot water and this, I can make the most delicious soup. You can try some if you don't believe me," he told her.

Mrs Skippen was so curious that she let Rob into her kitchen. He dropped the stone into a big pot of water that was boiling on the fire. After a while, he took a wooden spoon and had a sip from the pot.

"Is it ready?" asked Mrs Skippen.

"Nowhere near," said Rob. "It's a shame I don't have a carrot to help bring out the flavour."

"I've got a carrot!" said Mrs Skippen.

She fetched Rob a carrot from her pantry. He sliced it up and popped it into the pot. Then he took another sip.

"Is it ready?" asked Mrs Skippen.

"Coming along nicely," said Rob. "It could do with a bit of onion, though."

"I've got an onion!" said Mrs Skippen.

She went into her pantry and came out with an onion, which Rob sliced and put into the pot. Then he took another sip.

"Is it ready?" asked Mrs Skippen.

"Just about," said Rob. "But it's missing something. I always think that stone soup tastes better with some chicken in it."

"I've got a chicken!" said Mrs Skippen.

She brought a plump chicken from the pantry. Rob chopped it up, put it in the pot and stirred it round. Before long the kitchen was filled with a wonderful smell.

Rob dished the soup out into two bowls. When Mrs Skippen tasted it, it was so delicious that her eyebrows went up to the top of her head and the toes of her shoes curled right over.

"This is the best soup I've ever eaten!" she said. "And just think, it was made with a stone!"

"Not just any old stone," said Rob. "A soup stone."

"I wish I had a stone like yours!" sighed Mrs Skippen. "Then I could have stone soup every day."

"I'll tell you what," said Rob, helping himself to a second bowlful, "I'll let you have mine. I know where I can get another."

Mrs Skippen was so pleased that when

Rob had emptied his second bowl, she gave him a third.

When Rob left Waffam later that afternoon, he had a full stomach and a light heart – and when he looked behind, he saw that his shadow fitted him perfectly.

12

The Boasting Competition

It was a warm summer's evening, and a large crowd had gathered outside *The Speckled Toad* in the centre of Waffam to see the grand finale of the Annual Boasting Competition.

All day, the best boasters in the village had spun their yarns and told their tales until only three were left.

"Luke Tree is bound to win!" said Mrs Coral to her neighbour, Mrs Aspen.

"No he won't!" said Sam Pole, who was standing behind her. "Ben Blue is the best boaster in Waffam."

"Ben Blue is nowhere near as good a boaster as Walter Peak!" said Ned Pole.

"Yes he is!" said Sam.

"No he isn't!" said Ned.

The three boasters were seated at a table. The innkeeper brought them mugs of ale to whet their whistles.

"It's been a long, hot day," the innkeeper said as he set the mugs down on the table.

"Hot?" said Luke. "Why, when I was young, the summers were so hot, I used to take my clothes off and run around bare from dawn until dusk."

"Call that hot?" said Ben. "When I was a lad, the summers got so hot, my friends and I took off all our clothes and our skin, and played about in our skeletons."

Lazy Jack and his mother gasped at this.

"Only as hot as that?" said Walter. "The

summers were so hot when I was young, my brothers and I melted. Our dad had to put us in a bucket, carry us all the way up to the top of the mountain and pour us out on the snow, until we froze solid again."

"Ooh!" cried Polly, Tam and their three little ones.

"Talking about snow puts me in mind of the winters we used to have when I was a boy," said Luke. "It was so cold that when we milked our cow, she gave ice-cream."

"We never used to have ice-cream," said Ben. "We ate words instead. It was so cold in winter, when we spoke the words froze and fell on the floor. We used to pick 'em up and lick 'em."

"That's pretty cold," nodded Walter, "but not as cold as it used to get round our way. Our shadows stuck to the ice. We had to roll them up and pop them in the woodshed until spring came."

Mr and Mrs Vinegar clapped
when they heard this and
the rest of the crowd
joined in.

"Of course," said Luke, when the applause
had died down, "we didn't have ice-cream
every day. Most of the time, there was
nothing to eat but porridge. My old ma used
to make it in a kettle, and we'd take turns
sucking it up through the spout."

"We only had porridge as a special treat at
Christmas," said Ben. "The rest of the year,
all we had to eat was pea soup. Ma used to

make it with a saucepan of water and just one pea."

"We only had water," said Walter. "A dish of cold water soup in summer, and when we needed a hot meal in winter, Ma boiled the water and we used to eat the steam."

"Cor!" gasped Dan and Daisy.

"Funny you should mention steam," said Luke, "because my first job was working for a rich man who had a pair of steam-driven trousers because he was too proud to walk. I had to shovel coal into the boiler inside his left pocket, and it was hard work, I can tell you!"

"That's nothing compared to my first job," said Ben. "I had to walk round a forest in autumn, picking up all the fallen leaves. Then I spent the winter painting them green so they could be stuck back on the trees in spring."

"Sounds easy to me!" said Walter. "My first job was working in a desert. I had to count and number every grain of sand, and if there was ever a storm, I had to put the grains back in the right order."

Cheering broke out from the crowd, and Mr Plummer, the judge of the Boasting Competition, stood up to announce the result.

"I award the prize to all of you," he said. "I can't make up my mind who is the biggest boaster out of the three."

"I knew a chap once who couldn't make up his mind," said Luke. "He spent his whole life in bed because he couldn't decide which side of the bed to get out on."

"Call that not being able to make up your mind?" scoffed Ben. "You never met my Uncle Fogerty! Why, he used to spend so much time trying to make his mind up. . ."

The three boasters were off again, and there was no stopping them. They talked the moon up into the sky, they talked the legs off all the tables and chairs, and then they talked the moon out of the sky, and it was so dark that everybody went to sleep.

Outroduction

So, now you know. You've been to Waffam and you've met some of the people who live there. Now you have to be careful and keep an eye on yourself because some of the silliness might have rubbed off on you. Watch out for the telltale signs. Beware of chickens on the bus. Don't talk to signposts. If you're walking in the park and you see a cat riding a bicycle, go straight home, lie down and repeat the rhyme over the page until you feel more sensible.

Three wise men of Waffam
Went to sea in a bowl
If the bowl had been stronger
My tale would be longer